World of Insects

Praying Mantises

by Connie Colwell Miller

Consultant:
Gary A. Dunn, MS, Director of Education
Young Entomologists' Society Inc.
Lansing, Michigan

Capstone press
Mankato, Minnesota

Bridgestone Books are published by Capstone Press,
151 Good Counsel Drive, P.O. Box 669, Mankato, Minnesota 56002.
www.capstonepress.com

Library of Congress Cataloging-in-Publication Data
Miller, Connie Colwell, 1976–
    Praying mantises /by Connie Colwell Miller.
    p. cm.—(Bridgestone books. World of insects)
    Includes bibliographical references and index.
    ISBN 0-7368-3710-8 (hardcover)
    1. Mantodea—Juvenile literature. 2. Praying mantis—Juvenile literature. I. Title.
II. Series: World of insects.
QL505.83.M55 2005
595.7'27—dc22   2004014835

Summary: A brief introduction to praying mantises, discussing their characteristics, habitat, life cycle,
    and predators. Includes a range map, life cycle illustration, and amazing facts.

Editorial Credits

Erika L. Shores, editor; Jennifer Bergstrom, designer; Erin Scott, Wylde Hare Creative, illustrator;
    Jo Miller, photo researcher; Scott Thoms, photo editor

Photo Credits

Bill Johnson, 20
Brand X Pictures, back cover
Digital Vision, cover, 1, 12
Dwight R. Kuhn, 4, 6, 16
James P. Rowan, 10
Pete Carmichael, 18

1 2 3 4 5 6 10 09 08 07 06 05

Table of Contents

Praying Mantises

Praying mantises got their name because of the way they hold their legs. Praying mantises often bend their long front legs. They fold their legs close to their bodies. Many people think they look like they are praying.

Praying mantises are insects known for their strange looks. They may look like a plant stem or a flower. Praying mantises may look strange, but they have the same body parts as other insects. They have six legs and a hard outer covering called an **exoskeleton**.

◄ Praying mantises bend their front legs.

What Praying Mantises Look Like

Praying mantis bodies have three sections called the head, **thorax**, and **abdomen**. Praying mantises have a head shaped like a triangle. The two **antennas** on their head smell food. Their large eyes allow praying mantises to see very well.

Six legs and four wings join to the middle part of their bodies called the thorax. The wings cover the end section called the abdomen. A female praying mantis holds eggs in its abdomen.

◀ Praying mantises are about as long as your finger.

Praying Mantis Range Map

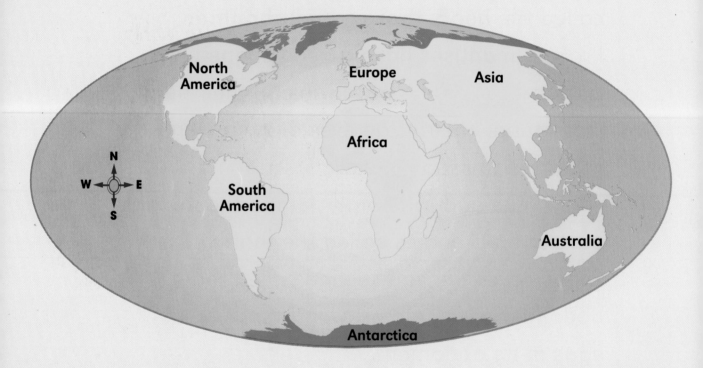

Where Praying Mantises Live

Praying Mantises in the World

About 2,000 types of praying mantises live in the world. Praying mantises live mainly in warm places. Most kinds of praying mantises live in tropical rain forests. Praying mantises find plenty of insects to eat in the rain forests.

◄ Praying mantises live in many places around the world.

Praying Mantis Habitats

Praying mantises find food and shelter in areas where plants grow. Praying mantis **habitats** are in meadows, grasslands, and rain forests.

Praying mantises look like the plants they live on. Praying mantises that live on flowers look like flowers. Praying mantises that live on leaves look like leaves.

◄ The orchid mantis lives on the orchid flower.

What Praying Mantises Eat

Praying mantises are **predators**. The insects they hunt are called prey. Praying mantises eat bees, grasshoppers, flies, moths, and other insects. Praying mantises use their powerful front legs to strike out and grab their prey.

Praying mantises can be **cannibals**. Cannibals eat their own kind. Female praying mantises may eat male praying mantises. Young praying mantises also eat each other.

◀ A praying mantis grabs and holds its prey with its front legs.

Life Cycle of a Praying Mantis

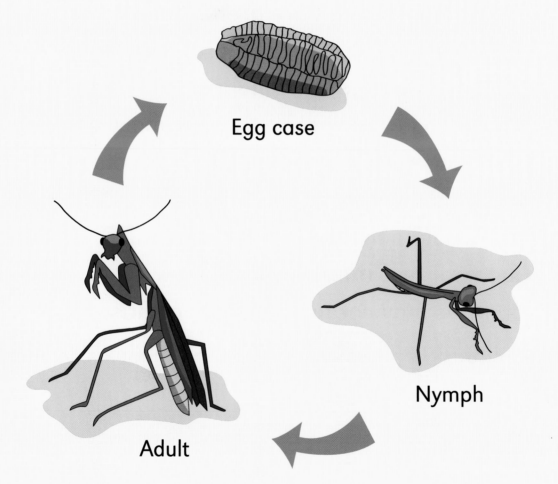

Egg case

Nymph

Adult

Eggs and Nymphs

Male and female praying mantises mate in late summer. The female praying mantis then lays its eggs on twigs and branches. It squirts a liquid onto the eggs. The liquid hardens into a case around the eggs. The case protects the eggs.

In spring, **nymphs** hatch from the eggs. Nymphs look like adult praying mantises, but they are smaller and don't have wings.

Molting into Adults

After hatching, a nymph begins to eat and grow. The nymph soon grows too large for its outer covering. The nymph then begins to **molt.** Its outer covering cracks open, and the nymph crawls out.

During summer, nymphs molt several times until they are full-grown. Their wings and other adult body parts develop the last time they molt. The nymphs are then adult praying mantises. They can fly and mate.

◄ Nymphs molt to become adults.

Dangers to Praying Mantises

Praying mantises have some predators. Bats, birds, spiders, and even other praying mantises eat them.

Camouflage helps praying mantises avoid being eaten. Their coloring helps them blend into their surroundings. Predators cannot easily see them.

You can look for praying mantises in meadows and grassy areas near your home. But you may have to look closely. Camouflage makes it hard to find praying mantises.

◄ Predators may not see this praying mantis. It looks like a leaf.

Amazing Facts about Praying Mantises

- Even speedy insects like mosquitoes and flies must watch out for a praying mantis. A praying mantis can quickly strike out and catch these insects.
- The praying mantis is the only insect that can turn its head like a person.
- Praying mantises live from 3 to 12 months.
- Female praying mantises don't fly. The eggs in their abdomens make them too heavy to fly.

◄ A praying mantis cleans its legs after eating its prey.

Glossary

abdomen (AB-duh-muhn)—the end section of an insect's body

antenna (an-TEN-uh)—a feeler on an insect's head

camouflage (KAM-uh-flahzh)—the coloring or covering that makes animals look like their surroundings

cannibal (KAN-uh-buhl)—an animal that eats its own kind

exoskeleton (eks-oh-SKEL-uh-tuhn)—the hard outer covering of an insect

habitat (HAB-uh-tat)—the place and natural conditions in which plants and animals live

molt (MOHLT)—to shed an outer layer of skin, or exoskeleton, so a new exoskeleton can be seen

nymph (NIMF)—a young form of an insect; nymphs change into adults by molting several times.

predator (PRED-uh-tur)—an animal that hunts other animals for food

thorax (THOR-aks)—the middle section of an insect's body

Read More

Hipp, Andrew. *The Life Cycle of a Praying Mantis*. The Life Cycles Library. New York: PowerKids Press, 2002.

Scholl, Elizabeth J. *Praying Mantis.* Bugs. San Diego: KidHaven Press, 2004.

Internet Sites

FactHound offers a safe, fun way to find Internet sites related to this book. All of the sites on FactHound have been researched by our staff.

Here's how:
1. Visit *www.facthound.com*
2. Type in this special code **0736837108** for age-appropriate sites. Or enter a search word related to this book for a more general search.
3. Click on the **Fetch It** button.

FactHound will fetch the best sites for you!

Index